Prescription for *Living*

Prescription for *Living*

Dr. Dorothy Wagner

Fawcett Columbine • New York

A Fawcett Columbine Book
Published by Ballantine Books

Library of Congress Catalog Card Number: 89-91780

ISBN: 0-449-90472-5

Manufactured in the United States of America

First Ballantine Books Edition: April 1990
10 9 8 7 6 5 4 3 2 1

Prescription for *Living*

Everyone's life is a journey to the self.

Psychologists agree that our basic personalities are formed in the first seven years of life.

Parents provide both
heredity and environment. Ironic, isn't it?

We tend to treat ourselves as we were treated as children.

No matter what our age, the child continues to live within us.

Guilt feelings originate
at such a young age as to
make actual guilt impossible.

We are strongly motivated
by the needs that exist
at unconscious levels.

The person who is suffering from excessive guilt will unconsciously seek punishment.

For better or worse, we get what we think we deserve in our unconscious.

People who feel guilty may seek a marriage partner who will physically or emotionally abuse them.

*If you have to force a relationship, it may not be the best one for you.

If you are looking for rejection,
you can always find it.

* We <u>are</u> our own worst enemy.

Our lives are shaped by those who love us and those who refuse to love us.

✝ The family that you came from isn't as important as the family that you create.

Often we do not see things as they are.
We see things according to
our personal perceptions.

To succeed, it is necessary to see the world as it is and learn to live with it.

You better not compromise yourself.
You really <u>are</u> all you have.

Self-love (vanity) is not so vile a sin,
as self-neglect.

Shakespeare, Henry V (1598)

What, in your opinion, is good enough for you?

Where do you feel out of place?
With whom do you feel out of place?

What are you most afraid would
happen if . . .

*A child who does not feel loved
may become a conformist or a rebel.*

To understand a person you must know their life experiences.

Unhappiness and failure in personal relationships often result from misunderstandings and miscommunications.

Repressed anger is the
source of great pain for ourselves
and others.

We act out our repressed sense of inferiority by trying to humiliate or dominate others.

Guilt is the gift that you don't
want to be guilty of giving!

Harsh criticism of a person only deepens their problems because it makes their self-acceptance more difficult.

A poor self-image is the cause of most people's failure to reach their potential.

Our behavior and our degree of happiness equate to our self-image.

Love enables a child to develop
a sense of self-worth.

Don't compare yourself to others.
Recognize your own strengths.

Never lose your enthusiasm.

Never let anyone put limitations on your ambitions.

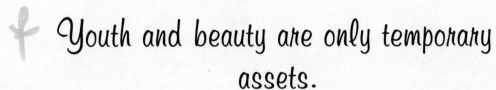

Youth and beauty are only temporary assets.

Education and experience can't
be taken away from you.

Beware of behavior that acts to relieve your tension rather than achieve your goal.

Don't you know not
making a decision is a decision?

If you don't know where you are going,
you may never get there.

Unless you move from the place where
you are you will always be there.

Our dreams propel us.
Our doubts anchor us.

We are the product of how we chose
to live our lives.

If you have to walk into a room containing a rattlesnake, would you rather have the light on or off?

Denial can be a dangerous
way of coping.

If you have a problem, it will continue as long as you refuse to acknowledge it.

Don't be afraid to take a
carefully thought-out risk.

Only a person who takes risks is free.

We each must take total responsibility for our own inner strength and development.

When you understand the meaning of life you will know what is truly important.